The New C...

By Liza Charlesworth

ISBN: 978-1-339-02785-2

Art Director: Tannaz Fassihi; Designer: Tanya Chernyak
Photos © Getty Images and Shutterstock.com.
1 2 3 4 5 6 7 8 9 10   68   32 31 30 29 28 27 26 25 24 23
Printed in Jiaxing, China. First printing, August 2023.

See the big jay!
She flew up to a branch
and chose to stay.

Then, she made a nest
and laid a few eggs.
Chicks were due in 15 days!

On cue, the shells broke.
Crack, crack! Pop, pop!
See the new chicks!

The new chicks were so cute!
Mom fed them seeds, bugs,
and snails. Gulp!

The chicks grew and grew.
In just a few weeks,
they jumped from the nest.

The jays got on top of a stick
and tried to use their wings.
Flap, flap! They did it!
They flew and flew.

They each flew to a tree
to make a new nest.
It's true they are not chicks.
They became big jays!